CL...
Bo...
Southwark Children
Centres

KU-604-448

美玲的呃逆

Mei Ling's Hiccups

By David Mills

Illustrated by Derek Brazell

Chinese translation by Sylvia Denham

lwich Wood Bookshop
J SEP 2008

SOUTHWARK LIBRARIES

SK 0562955 1

Mantra

「誰想玩集會遊戲？」美玲的老師問道。

"Who wants to play party games?" asked Mei Ling's teacher.

「跟著我呀！」他唱著。

"Follow me!" he sang.

但美玲想先把她的飲品飲完。
它真涼，
真好味，
她把最後的每一滴都喝乾！

But Mei Ling wanted to finish her drink.
It was cool
It was yummy
And she drank every last drop!

但當她喝完時，
她只能說：「呃！」

But when she'd finished
All she could say was ... "Hicc!"

另一個又來了：「呃！」
又另一個：「呃！」

And another one came: "Hicc!"
And another: "Hicc!"

「啊！不！」

Oh no!

彬吃吃地笑。
美玲也想笑，
但她只會説：「呃！」

Ben giggled.
Mei Ling wanted to laugh too
But all she could say was ... "Hicc!"

「我知道！我知道！」彬説，
「我的媽媽説你要這樣做…
然後數到五。」

"I know, I know!" said Ben.
"My mum says you have to do this...
and count to five."

So they both plugged their noses.
1 2 3 4 5 and ...
"HICC! Oh no!" said Mei Ling.

於是他們一起按著鼻子，
一 二 三 四 五 而…
「呃！啊！不！」美玲說。

跟著露比走進來，
「我知道！我知道！」露比說，
「我的爸爸說你要這樣做⋯」

Then Ruby came back in.
"I know, I know!" said Ruby.
"My dad says you have to do this ..."

So everyone tried to look upside down.
1 2 3 4 5 and ...
"HICC! Oh no!" said Mei Ling.

於是各人都嘗試顛上倒下的張望，
一 二 三 四 五 而 …
「呃…啊！不！」美
玲說。

跟著尼奧走進來，
「我知道！我知道！」尼奧說，
「我的叔叔說你要這樣做…」

Then Leo came back in.
"I know, I know!" said Leo.
"My uncle says you have to do this…"

於是各人從他們的
塑膠杯的另一邊喝水，
一 二 三 四 五 而 …
「呃…啊！不！」美玲說。

So everyone drank water from the other side
of their cups.
1　2　3　4　5　and …
"HICC! Oh no!" said Mei Ling.

跟著沙希走進來，
「我知道！我知道！」沙希說，
「我的祖母說你要這樣做…」

Then Sahil came back in.
"I know, I know!" said Sahil.
"My grandma says you have to do this..."

於是各人團團轉，團團轉，團團轉，
一　二　三　四　五　而…
「呃…啊！不！」美玲說。

So everyone went spin spin spin.
1　2　3　4　5　and ...
"HICC! Oh no!" said Mei Ling.

跟著蘇菲走進來，
「我知道！我知道！」蘇菲說，
「我的表哥說你要這樣做…」

Then Sophie came back in.
"I know, I know!" said Sophie.
"My cousin says you have to do this ..."

於是各人躺在地上做踏單車動作，
一 二 三 四 五 而 …
「呃…啊！不！」美玲説。

So everyone did bicycles in the air.
1 2 3 4 5 and ...
"HICC! Oh no!" said Mei Ling.

但她突然看到她的氣球，並想出一個主意，
「我知道，」她慢慢地說。
「美玲！」她的所有朋友都大聲叫。

But then she saw her balloon and she had an idea.
"I know," she said slowly.
"Mei Ling!" shouted all her friends.

砰！

美玲的氣球爆了。

POP!

went Mei Ling's balloon.

「噓！」各人小心地聽美玲的呃逆。

"Shhhhh!" Everyone listened carefully for Mei Ling's hiccups.

「沒有啦？」美玲細聲問道，

"Gone?" asked Mei Ling very quietly.

「沒有啦！」各人說。

"Gone!" said everyone.

「好哇！」各人大聲叫。

"HURRAY!" shouted everyone.

砰！ 砰！ 砰！ 砰！ 砰！ ...

POP! POP! POP! POP! POP! AND ...

「那是甚麼？」老師問道，

"What was that?" asked the teacher.

「呃！」各人説，
「啊！不！」美玲説。

"HICC!" said everyone.
"OH NO!" said Mei Ling.

For the children of Harry Roberts Nursery,
D.M.

For all the great children and staff of Soho Parish School,
and for Hilary, my lovely supportive mum, with love,
D.B.

Mantra Lingua
Global House
303 Ballards Lane
London N12 8NP
www.mantralingua.com

Text copyright © 2000 David Mills
Illustrations copyright © 2000 Derek Brazell
Dual language copyright © 2000 Mantra Lingua Ltd

First published in 2000 by Mantra Lingua Ltd
All rights reserved
This edition published 2007

A CIP record for this book is available from the British Library

Printed in Hong Kong